Cranes Arise

Cranes Arise
Haiku Scenes

GERALD VIZENOR

Nodin Press

ISBN: 0-931714-80-X

Nodin Press, a division of Micawber's , Inc.
525 North Third Street
Minneapolis, MN 55401

The drawing on the cover of this book is by Katsushika
Hokusai from his early nineteenth century *Mangwa* or
"Sketches at Random."

Japanese calligraphy is by Haruko Isobe.

In Memory of
Edward Copeland and George Mills

In the end I mended the rips in my pants,
replaced hat strings, and,
the moment I gave a moxa treatment to my kneecaps,
I thought of the moon over Matsushima.

Matsuo Basho, *Basho's Narrow Road*
Translated by Hiroaki Sato

The voice of a rooster rang out from the roof tops;
I fancied he was calling out to me to stop.
And it seemed as though the gentle wind that was rippling
through the growing wheat
was waving to me to come back.
So I finally rested my aching legs at the base of a tree,
and looked back along the way that I had come.

Kobayashi Issa, *The Year of My Life*
Translated by Nobuyaki Yuasa

AUTUMN

WINTER

SPRING

SUMMER

Cranes Arise is a collection of haiku scenes presented with place names, the actual locations of the original images. These imagistic scenes are meditative, the traces of nature, and create a sense of seasonal presence. This imagistic poem, for instance, was created at a restaurant in Ellsworth, Wisconsin.

> *fat green flies*
> *square dance on the pink grapefruit*
> *honor your partners*

The haiku scenes are arranged in the four seasons, a natural connection of imagist poems. The season is suggested in the first line of most haiku poems, as in *temple butterfly, curious crickets, first juncos, greedy mosquitos*, and *tricky frogs*. The second line of many haiku poems presents the action, the sense of motion, the natural reason and tension of the image, as in *master basho wades near shore, field mice rattle the dishes*, and *croak a haiku in the marsh*. The last line of a haiku poem teases a sense of presence, a sensation, and traces coincidence, consciousness, or contingency, as in *scent of rain, wings of a moth, geese alight, down to the sea*, and *skinny issa*.

"The essence of all nature poetry is animism," R. H. Blyth points out in *A History of Haiku*. "Haiku is an ascetic art, an artistic asceticism." Native animism is an artistic union of nature, images, and reason; the chance of visions by renunciation and meditation, and aesthetic sensibilities.

Kenneth Yasuda states in *The Japanese Haiku* that

haiku is an aesthetic experience, and that sense of a "*haiku moment*" is eternal. "Every word, then, in a haiku, rather than *contributing* to the meaning as words do in a novel or sonnet, *is* an experience."

Haiku scenes or *moments* are the actual aesthetic survivance of nature, the traces of artistic motion, and animistic associations: the imagistic scenes are more visionary than casuistic, mimetic, or solicitous; more descriptive than symbolic; more tricky than tetchy.

Haiku and native *anishinaabe* dream songs bear similar traces of animism, the seasons, and teases of natural reason. Haiku scenes and native dream songs are intuitive, meditative perceptions, and aesthetic survivance. Native memories are scenes of survivance, a visionary moment, an imagistic hush of natural reason.

Haiku poems are suggestive and "must be completed by the reader," writes Donald Keene in *Japanese Literature*. "What Japanese poets have most often sought is to create with a few words, usually with a few sharp images, the outline of a work whose details must be supplied by the reader, as in a Japanese painting a few strokes of the brush must suggest the whole world."

The first haiku scenes in each of the four seasons in this collection are suggestive of nature and, at the same time, tease the memories of three haiku poets. Matsuo Basho soaks his feet with the water striders in an autumn haiku scene, and wades with cranes in the spring. Yosa Buson comes to mind as mice run over the dishes in a winter haiku scene. Kobayashi Issa is teased in a summer haiku about tricky frogs.

Haiku or hokku scenes are distinctive phrases that "evolved out of *renga*," a linked poem that "flourished especially in the fourteenth and fifteenth centuries," Makoto Ueda writes in *Basho and His Interpreters*. Renga "was usually written by a team of poets under a set of prescribed rules." The first team wrote a hokku that suggested the season of the year, and the pattern of these hokku or haiku evolved as an independent poem in three phrases of five, seven, and five syllables. That exact syllable count, however, does not have the same meaning in other languages. Ueda translated this haiku by Basho:

> *in the seasonal rain*
> *a crane's legs*
> *have become short*

"There are three great names in the history of haiku, Basho, Buson, and Issa," writes R. H. Blyth in *Haiku: Eastern Culture*. "Basho is the religious man, Buson the artist, Issa the humanist." Basho is the poet in the very presence of nature. Buson is more objective and writes about "things as they exist by and for themselves, in their own right. Issa is concerned with man, man the weak angel; with birds and beasts as they struggle like us to make a living and keep their heads above water."

Basho was the "poet of life." Buson was the "poet

of the studio." Issa was the "poet of destiny," writes Blyth. "Basho, though his mind is tender and compassionate, has something resigned, something divine in him."

Matsuo Basho was born in 1644 at Ueno, near Kyoto. He was troubled, ridden by doubts as a youth, and then turned to Taoism and Zen Buddhism, writes Ueda. Basho decided on "*fuga*, an artist's way of life, a reclusive life devoted to a quest for eternal truth in nature." He pursued *fuga* with sincerity; nonetheless, "he had lingering misgivings about its redemptive power. To his last days, he did not seem able to merge poetry with belief completely."

Basho died on November 28, 1665. He "dictated this hokku to his student Donshu" three days before his death:

> *on a journey, ailing*
> *my dreams roam about*
> *on a withered moor*

"As it was a balmy day, many flies had gathered around the sliding screens, and the students were trying to catch them with a lime stick," writes Ueda. "Basho, amused that some were more skillful than others in handling the stick, laughed and said, 'Those flies seem delighted to have a sick man around unexpectedly.' He spoke no more. He breathed his last at around four that afternoon."

Yosa Buson was born near Osaka in 1716. The son of a farmer, he was educated in poetry and painting, a "brilliantly accomplished dilettante." Buson was "temperamentally incapable" of the devotion and intensities of Basho, observes Donald Keene in *World Within Walls*. "Despite his great admiration of Basho's poetry," Buson wrote that his poetry was "by no means directly imitated from Basho." Blyth translates this haiku by Buson:

> *winter rain*
> *a mouse runs*
> *over the koto*

"I enjoy changing my style from day to day as my fancy dictates," continues Buson in a translation by Keene. "I stay at home all the time, occupying myself with worldly matters, unable to accomplish any of the things I plan."

Buson, poor and troubled at the end of his life, "continued to write pictorially exquisite, absolutely unruffled poetry," writes Keene. "A letter written to a friend in 1777, describing his daughter's divorce," included this poem:

> *the rainy season*
> *the swollen river before them*
> *two little houses*

Keene points out that in "Buson's poetry, as in his paintings, realistic depiction was of little importance when compared to the nobility of the conception," as in this poem:

the evening breezes
the water splashes against
a blue heron's shins

Kobayashi Issa was born in Kashiwabara, a mountain village in central Japan, in 1763. His mother died when he was two years old; he was cared for by his grandmother, and then, eleven years later she died. Issa, at age thirteen, moved to Edo.

"Issa's whole life was a tragedy," writes Blyth in *Haiku: Eastern Culture*. "He was one of those men who attract failure and misfortune." Issa was moved by a sense of fate. "Life goes along joyfully and painfully, with ecstasy and anguish, and Issa goes with it. He does not praise or condemn."

for you fleas too
the night must be long
it must be lonely

"Issa's sympathies were always with small and weak animals, perhaps because he identified himself with them, as the victim of his stepmother's cruelty," writes Keene in *World Within Walls*.

skinny frog
don't be discouraged
issa is here

Japanese poets were once the warriors of impermanence, and many were actual road poets, a meditative, situational tradition of haiku literature. Basho traveled and wrote *haibun*, a distinctive form of prose and haiku, in his *Narrow Road to the Interior*.

Issa wrote haibun on his journey, *The Year of My Life*. "At long last I made up my mind to travel north," he writes in a translation by Nobuyuki Yuasa, "to get more experience in writing *haiku*. No sooner had I slung my beggar's bag round my neck and flung my little bundle over my shoulder than I noticed, to my great surprise, that my shadow was the very image of Saigyo, the famous poet-priest of times gone by." Saigyo was a twelfth century *waka* poet and priest.

"I knew well it was no use to cry, that water once flown past the bridge does not return, and blossoms that are scattered are gone beyond recall," Issa writes about the death of his daughter in *The Year of My Life*. "Yet try as I would, I could not, simply could not cut the binding cord of human love." Sato, his daughter, is remembered in this poignant haiku translated by Yuasa:

> the world of dew
> is the world of dew
> and yet . . .
> and yet . . .

Issa, at age fifty seven, wrote at the end of *The Year of My Life*, in December 1819, "Those who insist on salvation by faith and devote their minds to nothing else, are bound all the more firmly by their single-mindedness, and fall into the hell of attachment to their own salvation. Again, those who are passive and stand to one side waiting to be saved, consider that they are already perfect and rely rather on Buddha than on themselves to purify their hearts— these, too, have failed to find the secret of genuine salvation. The question then remains—how do we find it? But the answer, fortunately, is not difficult.

"We should do far better to put this vexing problem of salvation out of our minds altogether and place our reliance neither on faith nor on personal virtue, but surrender ourselves completely to the will of Buddha. Let him do as he will with us—be it to carry us to heaven, or to hell. Herein lies the secret."

Issa died eight years later. The frogs continue to croak his name, skinny Issa in the secret marsh, and he is celebrated by crickets, mosquitos, flies, many insects, and many birds. Issa is the eternal "poet of destiny."

Gerald Vizenor
Oakland, California

AUTUMN 秋

matsushima, japan

water striders
master basho wades near shore
out of reach

white earth, minnesota

redwing blackbird
rides the cattails at the slough
curtain calls

saint paul, minnesota

city squirrels
tease the calico house cat
at the window

santa fe, new mexico

cottonwood seeds
winded on the mountainside
float in a birdbath

saint paul, minnesota

autumn concert
oak leaves rush to the bandstand
one more encore

leech lake, minnesota

tricky squirrels
bounce over the maple boughs
last bright leaves

leech lake, minnesota

nervy crows
captain the moored sailboats
sound of thunder

berkeley, california

foggy morning
squirrels in the eucalyptus
cones resound

bemidji, minnesota

stout squirrel
hunkers on a willow branch
empty bird feeder

clear lake, minnesota

trickster moon
lingers behind a scarecrow
crown prince

mendocino cape, california

foggy morning
blue horses in the orchard
scent of apples

minneapolis, minnesota

northern juncos
tease the bare birch at sunrise
autumn ovation

leech lake, minnesota

midnight frost
moths flutter at the windows
out of breath

santa cruz, california

giant shadows
race across the meadow
horses at sunset

wenatchee, washington

ponderosa cones
scattered in a mountain storm
gather downstream

white earth, minnesota

october breeze
moves the shutters back and forth
wings of a moth

saint paul, minnesota

curious crickets
overnight in a downspout
out of tune

clear lake, minnesota

hoary scarecrow
whistles back at the stranger
crescent moon

bemidji, minnesota

bright leaves
gather with the sparrows
windy picnic

minneapolis, minnesota

painted hearts
decorate the river bridge
double crossed

WINTER 冬

kyoto, japan

giant snowflakes
alight in a cup of tea
buddhist temple

bena, minnesota

freezing rain
field mice rattle the dishes
buson's koto

minneapolis, minnesota

first snow
squirrels tie the trees together
double bows

cass lake, minnesota

ice floats
cast waves of sun on the lake
geese alight

grand marais, minnesota

white spruce
shoulder great mounds of snow
deer browse

clear lake, minnesota

birch firewood
double stacked behind the shed
smells of urine

menomonie, wisconsin

barn cats
return with the clumsy cows
for the milk

lake itasca, minnesota

winter rain
brightens the frozen sumac
sightly browse

pine point, minnesota

bright moon
shimmers in a natural nave
window ice

berkeley, california

winter storm
magnolias lose their past
faces overnight

minneapolis, minnesota

thirsty sparrows
gather around the new names
sunny gravestones

saint paul, minnesota

family diner
outlasted the train station
scent of cinnamon

grand marais, minnesota

timber wolves
raise their voices overnight
trickster stories

vietnam veterans memorial

columns of names
come alive in a snowstorm
sound of children

leech lake, minnesota

crusty snow
glistens in the early light
deer at the window

walker, minnesota

evening grosbeaks
overturn the birdfeeder
family feast

santa cruz, california

ocean storm
ravens ride the monterey pines
out of breath

minneapolis, minnesota

morning newspapers
stacked beneath the bay window
elevate the cat

cass lake, minnesota

ancient aspen
crashed on the river ice
scent of leaves

saint paul, minnesota

stately snowflakes
traces on the bay window
native lace

lake namakan, minnesota

birch leaves
caught in the river ice
wash ashore

chippewa national forest

snow chunks
tumble through the cedar boughs
spring stories

white earth, minnesota

wooden bucket
frozen under a downspout
springs a leak

minneapolis, minnesota

warm morning
mounds of dogshit in the snow
close to home

SPRING

lake itasca, minnesota

spring fever
basho wades in the shallows
cranes arise

oakland, california

march moon
shimmers over the sidewalk
snail traces

santa cruz, california

plum petals
decorate the black cat
garden party

minneapolis, minnesota

cold rain
children on their way to school
scent of lilacs

castle danger, minnesota

mounds of foam
downriver from the waterfall
float silently

gravesend, england

primroses
spring in a common garden
first nighter

white earth, minnesota

crescent moon
children stone the water tower
sound of crickets

saint paul, minnesota

bright ladybugs
parade on the birdfeeder
guarded by the cat

minneapolis, minnesota

cherry blossoms
catch a warm breeze on the pond
brighten the shore

bemidji, minnesota

white butterfly
waves on a plastic bouquet
bridal wreath

menomonie, wisconsin

apple blossoms
scatter the early rainlight
over the garden

minneapolis, minnesota

orange kitten
pounces on the dandelions
one at a time

minneapolis, minnesota

paper boats
sail on a crack of thunder
out to sea

saint cloud, minnesota

calico kittens
circle a saucer of milk
garden stones

minnetonka, minnesota

giant lilacs
bear the overnight rain
over the path

leech lake, minnesota

first juncos
pose in a bare birch tree
on their return

rosebud, south dakota

golden eagles
circle the great blue horses
prairie sunset

cass lake, minnesota

paper dragon
clatters high in a poplar
alone overnight

cannon falls, minnesota

morning glories
flourish on the broken fence
spring repairs

santa cruz, california

gentle rain
cat asleep in the window
doves in the eaves

saint croix falls, wisconsin

cherry blossoms
brighten the picnic table
thunderstorm

bemidji, minnesota

stick boats
set sail on the early tide
late for school

grand marais, minnesota

downy woodpecker
beats a tune on a dead tree
superior sonata

oakland, california

scruffy sparrows
chatter outside the bakery
birds of passage

SUMMER

夏

lake itasca, minnesota

tricky frogs
croak a haiku in the marsh
skinny issa

ellsworth, wisconsin

fat green flies
square dance on the pink grapefruit
honor your partners

beijing, china

china sunrise
tourists circle the statues
cicada fugues

berkeley, california

bird of paradise
leans over the cedar fence
bus stop poses

tokyo, japan

palace ravens
circle the restaurant trash
to the manner born

scenic, washington

red spider
marches over the cascades
mountain map

minneapolis, minnesota

horde of catkins
cornered in a thunderstorm
broken umbrella

kyoto, japan

temple butterfly
dithers on the smooth white stones
scent of rain

bena, minnesota

blue dragonflies
cross their wings in the cattails
sunrise service

blue earth, minnesota

old school bell
sounds once or twice a summer
hailstorm

half moon bay, california

nasturtiums
decorate the last fences
down to the sea

capitola, california

ocean sunset
sandpiper poses on one leg
giant shadow

madeline island, wisconsin

great clouds
scatter on tiny waves
skipping stones

oakland, california

fair wisteria
circle the old rose window
shadow play

bayfield, wisconsin

mighty pinwheels
shiver in a thunderstorm
party favors

saint paul, minnesota

willow leaves
down overnight in a storm
laurels at dawn

san gregorio, california

ant colonies
march over the sand castles
honor the dead

old frontenac, minnesota

bright clothespins
shimmy on the rusted line
thunderstorm

clear lake, minnesota

great blue heron
stands alone in the shallows
cat on the dock

park rapids, minnesota

early sunbursts
chase clouds over the meadow
crows on the wire

saint paul, minnesota

catalpa leaves
hold back the overnight rain
morning breeze

lake itasca, minnesota

moccasin flower
blossoms in the moist shadows
out of sight

grey eagle, minnesota

august hailstorm
marches across the corn field
row after row

minneapolis, minnesota

bright moon
bounces on the mississippi
wake of a canoe

maiden rock, wisconsin

calico cat
stumbles in the snapdragons
raucous crows

new prague, minnesota

tardy swallows
nest in the old school house
summer recess

berkeley, california

great poppies
turn out with every sunburst
near a bus stop

oakland, california

cold rain
an old woman walks her dog
scent of cedar

leech lake, minnesota

paper lanterns
tricked the party moths last night
sunrise stories

clear lake, minnesota

great blue heron
august dancer in the marsh
creak of oars

stevens pass, washington

water ouzel
dives in a cold mountain stream
out of breath

berkeley, california

child in the rain
holds a bright red parasol
over the roses

fort bragg, california

african daisies
shiver in an ocean storm
faces at bay

santa cruz, california

bright poppies
flower on a wet window
ocean storm

menomonie, wisconsin

cowbirds
ride the bossies to pasture
borrowed nests

maple lake, minnesota

fat mosquitos
ate too much at a picnic
crash in the grass

collegeville, minnesota

overnight storm
young monks wade in the puddles
natural breakaway

beaulieu, minnesota

grasshoppers
ride the linen on the line
late harvest

oakland, california

hummingbirds
court the african lilies
day after day

berkeley, california

august poppies
raise their heads in the sunshine
elders in the park

bean hollow state beach, california

sandpipers
run at the edge of the waves
legs lost in foam

san francisco, california

bridal wreath˙
butterflies wave to vizenor
high hopes